A
LOVELY
Couple

To Sarah & C.J —
remembering your [...]
anniversary in 2009.

May the Lord continue
to bless your sweet marriage
with HIS powerful Love and Truth.

In His Love,
your friend @ NABC,
Betsy Alem

a gift

for _____

from _____

Published in Nashville, Tennessee, by Thomas Nelson. Thomas Nelson is a registered trademark of Thomas Nelson, Inc.

Published in association with Yates & Yates, LLP Attorneys and Literary Agents, Orange, CA.

Some of the names used in scenarios in this book are not actual names; identifying details have been changed to protect anonymity. Any resemblance to persons alive or dead is purely coincidental.

Art Director: Kevin Swanson
Designer: Alison T. Bauer
Production Artist: Dan C. Horton

Thomas Nelson, Inc., titles may be purchased in bulk for educational, business, fund-raising, or sales promotional use. For information, please e-mail SpecialMarkets@ThomasNelson.com.

Unless otherwise noted, Scripture quotations are taken from The Holy Bible, New International Version®. © 1973, 1978, 1984 by International Bible Society. Used by permission of Zondervan. All rights reserved.

ISBN-13: 978-1-4041-0532-4

Printed in China

08 09 10 11 12 MT 6 5 4 3 2 1

simple secrets
OF a
great marriage

BY DR. HENRY CLOUD & DR. JOHN TOWNSEND

THOMAS NELSON
Since 1798

NASHVILLE   DALLAS   MEXICO CITY   RIO DE JANEIRO   BEIJING

table of contents

introduction

how to get the most marriage mileage out of this book

You may have picked up or received this book for any number of reasons, such as:

- You're in a good marriage, but you want it to be even better.

- You're scrambling for answers in your marriage, aware that it's nowhere near great at this point.

- You and your mate periodically work through a marriage book together to keep your relationship fine-tuned and humming.

- Your spouse handed the book to you with that look in his or her eye that says, "Get a clue."

- You're engaged, and a caring friend or relative wants you to get your upcoming marriage started on the right foot.

- You're widowed or divorced and intent on getting it right the next time.

No matter how or why you've ended up with this book in your hands, we're glad you're here. We want you to know that, wherever you're starting from, you've embarked on a twenty-one-secret journey that will, if you stick with us and do the work, make a great, positive difference in your marriage. We have shared these principles with literally thousands of people, and those who diligently worked them into their relationship have become better spouses and are enjoying great marriages. We're confident it will happen for you too.

But before you hit the road on this life-changing, marriage-improving journey, here are a few tips to help you get the most mileage from your effort.

You will benefit even if your partner doesn't read this book.

We think it's ideal that you and your spouse (or spouse-to-be) read the book and work through the exercises together. But if he or she isn't quite ready for that process, your marriage will still profit greatly if you start the journey alone. Great marriages result as each partner focuses on him- or herself, determined, with God's help, to be the best mate possible. As you grow through these principles, your marriage will likely improve even if your mate isn't with the program yet.

You will get the most mileage when you go beyond just reading.

At the end of each chapter you will find an application section headed *Think about It, Talk about It, Live It*. The questions and exercises we provide there are designed to help you translate principles for a great marriage into the day-by-day expression of your marriage.

If you are taking this journey as a couple, we suggest that you first read each chapter individually. Think through the application section, jot some notes, and decide how you personally will respond to the principle you've just read about. Then get together with your partner to share with each other your insights and responses from the chapter. Some couples might want to read chapters aloud to each other and talk through the exercises together instead of doing the work separately. That's okay, but we think you will find extra benefit from getting inside your own head and heart first, then coming together with some well-considered responses.

If you are taking this journey alone, don't skip the application section. Work through the questions and exercises as they apply to you, even if you can't share them with your spouse right now. If the opportunity arises to share with your partner from what you're reading, make sure it's about what God is doing in you, not what you think your partner needs to do. A great marriage is about changing yourself, not your mate.

Each chapter ends with a *Great Marriage Commitment*, crystallized from the chapter's theme. Consider concluding your discussion of each chapter by sharing this commitment—or something similar in your own words—with each other verbally. Then take a few moments to pray together, asking God to help you live out each great marriage commitment. If you are journeying alone, let God hear your heartfelt commitment to your spouse, then live out that commitment to His glory and the growing strength of your marriage.

You can explore the twenty-one secrets several ways.

If you wish, you can tackle a secret a day, embarking on a twenty-one-day journey of discovery. Of course, we're not saying that you have to clear your calendar for three weeks and blaze through this book a chapter per night in marathon fashion. It's great if you want to do that, but we're aware that the busy lives of most people won't afford them that luxury. We're really talking about exploring twenty-one principles for a great marriage in a logical sequence. Here are several ways to tackle a twenty-one-day approach:

If you and your partner are working through the book together . . .

• Set your own twenty-one-day schedule. For example, how about setting aside twenty-one consecutive Tuesday evenings or Saturday mornings? This gives each partner a week to read and work through the next chapter, priming you for a thoughtful, prayerful discussion of each principle. Or perhaps you can set aside two or three evenings each week. The schedule you choose should allow each of you unhurried time for personal reading and thinking before you talk.

• Consider taking the journey in twenty-one weeks with another couple or a small group of couples. For example, do the work as individuals and a couple, as suggested above. Then meet with your small group one evening a week to talk about each couple's progress, encourage one another, pray for one another, and hold each other accountable.

• Plan a great marriage vacation or retreat just for the two of you. If you have the means to do so, get away for a week and work through the book in a concentrated fashion, dealing with three chapters a day for seven days. Or perhaps set up a series of weekend retreats—one per month or so—and tackle two or three chapters each weekend. Maybe another couple or two would like to join you on these marriage-building retreats.

If you are beginning this journey without your spouse, you can select a pace that best suits your schedule and needs. If a measure of accountability will help you stay disciplined and keep you on pace, think about meeting periodically with a friend or small group of friends who will work through the book with you. Just don't let your spouse become uncomfortable and suspect you are talking about him or her and your marriage. You can simply say something like, "I'm meeting with some girlfriends to discuss how we can be better wives to our husbands."

Your marriage can become greater and greater and greater . . .

The intent of this book is not to "certify" your marriage as "great"— the way you earn a diploma, a degree, a merit badge, a black belt, or any other certification of mastery. A "great marriage" is an ongoing process, not a plateau of achievement. We hope you can say at the end of this book that your marriage is better than it was when you started. But we hope you never say that your marriage is as great as it can be and there is no room for improvement.

Work through this journey again six months or a year from now. Read other good materials about marriage. Attend marriage-enrichment classes and conferences. Never stop growing into the mate God designed you to be.

simple secret 1

grow
your marriage
to greatness

How do you feel as you take this first step

to a more fulfilling marriage? Hopeful?

Energized? Doubtful? Skeptical? All pretty

normal emotions at this point. No matter how

you feel, we encourage you to not underestimate

God's power to make a positive difference

in your relationship, beginning today.

"When I was single, I was unhappy and insecure. Then I married Ron and became married, unhappy, and insecure," said my friend Denise, whom I (John) had not seen in several years.

"Even though at first it was depressing to realize that," she continued, "it really helped me to understand that my failure to be happy was my own problem. If I expected to be happy, I had some growing up to do."

Denise's insight introduces the vital point we must make right from the get-go. Emotional, spiritual, and relational growth is the cornerstone to enjoying a solid and happy marriage. If you are not open to growth— both as individuals and as a married couple—your marriage will fall far short of what you want it to be.

In Marriage, Growth Trumps Happiness

Many couples are swept up in the fantasy that happiness is the supreme goal of marriage. Now, there is certainly nothing intrinsically wrong with wanting to be happy. Happiness is a good and positive thing, and a gift from God. Psalm 68:3 says, "But may the righteous be glad and rejoice before God; may they be happy and joyful." But in reality, *happiness is not a good goal for life or marriage.* A much better goal is *growth*, and one of the by-products of growth is happiness.

The spiritual and emotional growth process, designed by God, is about discovering what we lack inside, where we are empty, and where we've been damaged emotionally, psychologically, and even spiritually. We find out how unfinished we are and how much we need God and others, including our spouse. But growth doesn't stop there. The next step is experiencing the many ways we can be filled, matured, and healed. When we begin addressing our needs for growth, we find happiness.

Don't ask from marriage the happiness that only personal growth can provide. Instead, focus on growing out of whatever is keeping you from being the fulfilled and complete person you need to be. The result: your marriage will become a wonderful haven of love, connection, intimacy, passion, and happiness. Growing people create growing, happy marriages.

Another benefit of pursuing your own growth is that *growing people tend to be attractive people*. For instance, when a woman becomes compassionate, she can show compassion to her spouse. When she becomes honest, she can give and receive truth with her spouse. When she has experienced that it is okay to be real and imperfect, she can accept reality and imperfection in him. When she can look into deeper parts of her own soul, she can help make it safe for him to reveal his deeper self to her.

This kind of personal growth frees partners from feeling responsible for the happiness and fulfillment of each other. That is a huge weight to get rid of. A friend once told her husband, "I'm sorry for making you responsible for making me happy. That is my problem, not yours. I do want things from you, and I want to give you good things too. But I'm taking this one over for myself." The husband's jaw dropped. He couldn't believe it wasn't all his fault anymore. And their relationship improved dramatically.

How to Start a Growing Marriage

Here are some ways to launch your marriage in the direction of greatness—and happiness:

Ask each other if your marriage is burdened with the "happiness fantasy." Has one of you been expecting the other to "make me happy and fulfilled"? Or is one of you blaming the other for personal unhappiness? If the "happiness fantasy" is alive and well in your marriage, agree together that the fantasy must die so that real love can live.

Commit yourselves to the growth process. As a couple, decide that you will both commit to personal and spiritual growth. You can't make a marriage grow if you're not deeply invested in your own personal growth. Realize that the growth process will take time, energy, involvement, and probably the help of other people. But by all means, budget your commitments to be sure you allow time for each other.

Become companions to each other's growth. The best attitude couples can adopt is that of two companions: *I will support your growth, and you will support mine. We are not responsible for each other's growth process, but we will help and encourage each other in it.* Remember, a growing person is an attractive, interesting, encouraging, and passionate person. As you grow, you and your spouse should become aware that you are both getting a really good deal!

1 The marriage fantasy says, *My spouse should make me happy.*
  Be honest: to what degree have you bought into this fantasy?

2 What setting and context would best foster your personal growth?
  Your growth together?

3 How will you convey to your partner today your commitment to
  personal growth and marriage growth (eye-to-eye statement, sticky
  note on the bathroom mirror, e-mail)? Feel free to use or adapt
  the statement below.

great marriage commitment 1

*With God's help, I will steadfastly pursue my own spiritual and emotional growth,
thus encouraging growth and happiness in our marriage.*

simple secret 2

---

accept
each other
no matter what

You've reached step two—it's a good

sign that you really are committed to each other

and to growing a great marriage. And we're

committed to helping you get there. Let's tackle

head-on how a great marriage deals with

the obvious imperfections and shortcomings

each partner brings to the relationship.

I (John) was having dinner with Dan and Stephanie, friends who have been married a long time. They have always seemed close to each other. The conversation turned to their early days as a couple. They talked about the challenges they had resolved, which resulted in the good place they were in now.

Stephanie said, "I was so mad at Dan for a long time. I thought he was the most unaccepting, unloving, critical person I had ever met, and I wondered how we ever got together."

Dan laughed. "I remember those days. I was such the bad guy."

"So what's the deal?" I asked.

"When we were dating," Stephanie said, "he seemed really caring and compassionate. But after we got married, all of a sudden he started talking about things that were wrong with me—that I wasn't keeping up the apartment and the finances. Dan was pretty much right about those things. It bothered him, and he didn't use the kindest words to tell me about it."

Stephanie continued. "I thought that if Dan really accepted me, he would live with these things. But after a lot of talking about it, I finally realized that it wasn't about accepting me. It was about expecting things of me. I saw those two things as the same. But I finally got it that they were different, and things got better."

Acceptance and Love

Stephanie and Dan's early days are a good starting point to understand what acceptance means in love and romance. Acceptance is one of the primary ingredients for healthy intimacy and a great marriage, yet there is a lot of misinformation and wrong thinking about it.

Acceptance is a term often used to mean that your love is so great and so deep that there is nothing the two of you can do that will really disturb or distance each other. Where acceptance exists, all can be forgiven and forgotten, in the name of love. If you want a great marriage, acceptance will play a large role. *In fact, the extent to which you love your partner is the extent to which you accept him or her.*

When we accept someone, we receive that person into our heart. We take in all parts, all aspects, all realities—good, bad, and immature. That's the kind of acceptance God gives to us—and that we in turn give to our partner. In response to acceptance, we "accept one another, then, just as Christ accepted you, in order to bring praise to God" (Romans 15:7).

Acceptance is important because no one can love, trust, or grow without knowing that he or she has been drawn close, warts and all, by another person. If your mate feels that some part of him or her isn't good enough for you, for example, he or she will disconnect, get angry, or pretend to be someone else. And the two of you will not experience the fullness of love.

All growth begins with acceptance; without it we just hide and pretend, hoping to avoid the disappointment and wrath of our partner. Only in the light and freedom of acceptance can you talk about, process, pray, and support—and develop solutions for your weaknesses and issues.

Approval and Agreement

A major misconception about acceptance is that it conveys approval or unconditional agreement. Sometimes a partner will demand that an action or attitude must be approved for the other to be seen as an accepting person. This is not true, and it doesn't work in relationships.

If you approve of or agree with something bad, immature, or wrong, you are contributing to more of the same, which is most likely what you'll continue to get. For example, suppose your partner has friends you don't approve of. They don't support your relationship, and they aren't good for your spouse. For you to approve of or agree with these friendships is to give license to something that could hurt your connection and intimacy. You may accept that they are important friends, and you don't need to judge them for their attitude. But you don't have to approve of or tolerate behavior or influence that could be bad for you as a couple.

When approval or agreement issues arise, be as accepting, humble, loving, and open as you can be. But whatever you do, *do not give up your position*, as long as it is healthy and reasonable. You want growth and improvement. To love and accept each other totally, you must care enough to confront.

1 In what ways, if any, are you—or might you seem to be— unaccepting of your partner? When, if at all, do you feel unaccepted by your partner?

2 Write a brief note to your partner expressing one element of appreciation or concern on the topic of acceptance in your marriage. Craft your words in the context of your ongoing love and commitment to him or her.

great marriage commitment 2

With God's help, I will demonstrate my total acceptance of you, even when I disagree with or disapprove of your behavior.

simple secret ♥ 3

---

focus
on changing
yourself,
not
your mate

Now that you have your feet solidly planted

on the two cornerstones for a great marriage—

growth and acceptance—let's focus on "I" skills

for a while. A little self-examination and personal

growth will pay big dividends in your marriage.

How would you assess the future of your marriage if you knew that your partner's behavior, attitudes, habits, manner of speaking, and manner of responding to you were never going to change? You might think, *This is depressing. I'm supposed to settle for the way things are and try to be happy anyway? That's not my idea of a great marriage.*

Your relationship might be fairly healthy, or it may be in trouble—or even in crisis. And perhaps your mate shoulders a large share of the blame for your less-than-ideal situation. Whatever the case, the best thing you can do right now to turn your marriage in the direction of greatness is to focus on yourself, not on your spouse. Good things can happen to the relationship when you start working on yourself instead of trying to change your mate.

Health Breeds Health

For years, I (John) had chronic lower back pain due to a sports injury. The traditional treatments of rest, stretches, massage, and cold and heat didn't help. But one day, at a backyard barbecue, an engineer told me, "Your back is like a suspension bridge. To strengthen it, you have to strengthen the supportive structures around it—the muscles that hold it together." He suggested a regimen of daily sit-ups. I followed his advice, and within a few months, my pain was gone.

I don't really understand the engineering behind it, but I do know that when I concentrated on improving one part of my body, the other part improved too. In the same way, your marriage is like that body system. Things you do individually matter to the relationship. And generally speaking, *you can do more to improve your relationship than you think.*

The Bible explains this in terms of being a person of light—that is, one who follows God's light of love, relationship, and growth. "In the same way, let your light shine before men, that they may see your good deeds and praise your Father in heaven" (Matthew 5:16). Light tends to spark a response in other people, including your spouse. Let's look at the three key things you can do yourself and bring good light to your connection.

You can add healthy ingredients to the marriage. When you make yourself vulnerable to your partner, instead of resenting and nagging, you will introduce good ingredients of growth into your marriage. By working on changing yourself, you make openness, trust, safety, and even change easier for your mate. You also need to get rid of negative ingredients such as distance, stonewalling, and blame—even when they seem justified.

When you shine the light on your own life and attitudes, you add growth and health not only to yourself but also to your marriage. You may not see instant results. That's okay. Start making healthy, positive choices in your life. Get to know yourself, each other, and God in a deeper way.

You can influence your mate. Not only does changing yourself bring good things to your marriage, but it also helps you influence your partner to change and grow. Sometimes we try to control our spouses and force a change. Reality check: you cannot make anyone change; your mate always has a choice. So give up control. Influence is much more helpful than coercion. You model, give information, make requests, and are vulnerable and safe—and seek to respect your spouse's choices.

However, don't be afraid to put the *right kinds* of pressure on your spouse. Talk to him or her. Say, "I love you, and our growth as a couple is important to me." Healthy pressure is growth-producing pressure.

You can recruit your mate to help you. The healthiest marriages are those in which both partners commit to personal growth and change, working on themselves and doing their respective roles. Use this image: you're in a boat and each of you paddles on your own side of the boat and contributes to the progress of the marriage.

Recruit your mate to the team concept. Talk about what you both want together: more connection, more safety, more emotional intimacy, more vulnerability, more honesty, a greater sense of teamwork, and a more satisfying sexual relationship. Talk about how you affect each other. Then shoulder the burdens of changing yourself in the right ways.

think about it | talk about it | live it

1 Good things can happen in a relationship when you start working on *you*. What might be your first step in "working on *you*"?

2 Whenever you catch yourself thinking, *How can I change myself?*—instead of thinking, *How can I change my partner?*—reward yourself in a simple way (such as putting a quarter in a jar, saving up for lunch out for two). But only if you act on your good thought!

great marriage commitment ❤3

With God's help, I will focus on my part in enriching our marriage by focusing on positive changes I need to make in my behavior and attitudes.

simple secret 4

set
self
aside

Have you ever found it difficult to make

needed changes in yourself for the good

of your marriage? It's time to meet that obstacle

in person: it's you! We know because we battle

"self" in our own marriages. So let's take

"self" to the mat together.

Remember the days before you were married? Remember the freedom of doing whatever you wanted, whenever you wanted? You answered only to yourself, and that was pretty much it.

Then you fell in love. All of a sudden you had to say no to yourself with respect to freedoms, choices, and preferences that you enjoyed in your previous life. You had to consider someone else's feelings and desires, which can be a painful way of life.

This way of life is called self-denial. Simply put, self-denial is *the practice of postponing, or even giving up, activities and attitudes that block love and connection.* In great marriages, self-denial is a daily way of living, relating, and thinking. And it is one of the most important keys to love.

Take Off the Headphones

Self-denial creates the space you both need for love to grow. The more you understand healthy self-denial, the more you will truly love and give to your mate. And don't be surprised when your partner responds in kind!

Think of it this way. Suppose you want to talk to your mate about something, but *someone's* wearing those noise-canceling headphones and listening to music on the MP3 player. You ask your question but you get only a quizzical glance in response. Your mate can't hear a word you're saying. But when he or she sees that you want to talk and takes off the headphones, you can communicate and be together.

In the same way, we all tend to focus on our own feelings, opinions, dreams, hurts, needs, and wants. Self-denial is the mechanism that helps you shut off the MP3 player in your head. It allows you to say no, sometimes temporarily and sometimes permanently, to things you are focusing on. As a result, you create space to hear and respond to your mate's wants and needs.

When couples learn to deny themselves, they experience a wonderful and transcendent mystery of love: *When I deny "me," I connect with "us."* To let go of a wish or demand for the sake of the relationship puts you into a new kind of life: the life of "us." This life is far superior to the life of "me." "I" serves "we"—and is the better for it.

What Self-Denial Looks Like

A loving and well-considered attitude of self-denial will mean giving up things like these:

The comfort of detachment. Love requires the effort of making an emotional connection, even when you least feel like it. It's very natural to disconnect when you're stressed, tired, or upset with your spouse, and at times you do need "me" time. But more often, you need to deny yourself the choice of withdrawing from the relationship. Getting out of your comfort zone and connecting on the relationship's terms, not your own, helps generate love and close feelings.

Your dreams and desires. At times, one partner will need to postpone a worthwhile dream or legitimate desire for the sake of the connection. For example, a wife might delay developing her career while she raises the kids. Or a husband might live in a city that is not best for his career but best for the marriage and family.

The right to demand fairness. When both partners insist on playing fair, they enter into legalistic, loveless emptiness. Give more than you receive in your love life, and deny yourself the demand for fairness. Don't get miffed if you end up going to the basketball game with him more than he goes to the symphony with you. Love gives up keeping score in order to build connection and compassion.

Saying whatever you want. Learn to deny the strong urge to say to your mate exactly what you feel, at the moment you feel it. Partners hurt each other deeply when they assume they have *carte blanche* to say anything to each other. Instead, first ask yourself, "How would I feel if my love said that to me?" This sort of approach also includes denying yourself the privilege of confronting every little thing your mate does. As Proverbs 19:11 says, "A man's wisdom gives him patience; it is to his glory to overlook an offense."

Self-denial is like the economic laws of saving and investing money: those people who can be patient and wait will always reap the greatest payoffs in the long run.

think about it | talk about it | live it

1 The chapter states, *When I deny "me," I connect with "us."*
   What taste, if any, of "the life of us" have you experienced?
   Give an example.

2 Which of the five expressions of self-denial mentioned earlier
   will you work on in order to practice "a loving and well-
   considered attitude of self-denial"?

3 Give yourself a secret self-denial assignment (that's right—don't
   call attention to it) this week, such as serving your spouse's morning
   coffee before you serve yourself, or taking on one of the chores your
   spouse usually does. See how he or she responds.

great marriage commitment 4

*With God's help, I will grow in my willingness and ability to postpone or give up
activities and attitudes that block love and connection between us.*

simple secret 5

grow
out of
your
immaturity

Congratulations on reaching step five!

Whether you sense it or not, you are well on

your way to building a great marriage. Another

self-focusing step in the process is dealing with

vestiges of immaturity. So read on . . .

and grow up where you need to.

Dave and Stacy had come to my (John's) office for marriage counseling. After listening to their stories, I finally said, "Dave, if you want the marriage I think you want, you're going to have to take a hard look at your immaturity and deal with it."

Dave eyed me skeptically. "What do you mean 'immaturity'?"

"Well, for example, I don't see that you put a great deal of effort into seeing Stacy's side of things. But at the same time, you expect her to see yours. We were talking a few minutes ago about Stacy feeling disconnected from you because you bought the boat without consulting her. Listen as Stacy tells you how she feels when you don't hear her side of things."

Dave agreed, and Stacy turned to him. "When I try to tell you that the boat makes me feel like we're going to be financially unstable, and you get mad at me for bringing it up, I lose all hope that we'll make it." Then she choked up and stopped.

Dave's face changed. Stacy's vulnerability took him by surprise, and his eyes filled with tears. "Honey, I didn't know you were scared," he said, leaning toward her. "I thought you were just upset with me. I'm so sorry."

Our conversations continued in subsequent sessions. Gradually Dave became more aware of his immaturity and progressed in resolving it. The key was in seeing how deeply his immaturity affected Stacy. That helped him keep moving ahead.

What Is Immaturity?

To be immature is to be incomplete or underdeveloped. In terms of emotional and personal growth, immaturity means that an individual has not yet become an adult in the full sense of the word. Immature attitudes affect one's ability to love, relate, care, and build good relationships. Here are some of the most common immature attitudes:

Detachment. The detached partner either distances him- or herself mentally or focuses on other things, causing the other partner to feel alone and disconnected.

Control. When one spouse resists the other's freedom, the issue is control, which is also a type of immaturity. An immature partner, for example, attempts to make his spouse do things his way, often by using intimidation, aggressiveness, manipulation, or guilt.

Irresponsibility. One sign of a mature marriage is that both spouses are responsible and faithful to the relationship. A partner who fails to "own" his or her responsibilities is demonstrating immaturity, being undependable and unreliable.

Self-centeredness. Adults should be able to step out of their own point of view and enter the world of others' feelings, values, experiences, and opinions. When a spouse does not readily engage at this level, the immaturity of self-centeredness is often the cause.

Immaturity causes imbalance, loss of safety and love, and negative feelings in a marriage. When one spouse is immature, the other feels like a burdened and resentful parent of a selfish child.

Deal with Immaturity Now

The good thing about immaturity is that it's not an incurable disease. The right treatment will get rid of it. Here are two ways to deal with immaturity.

Look at your own immaturity first. The happiest couples are those in which the individual members first focus on how they themselves are showing immaturity. As Jesus taught, everyone needs to "first take the plank out of your own eye" before judging someone else (Matthew 7:5). This is what love is all about. You want to preserve, help, and grow the relationship—and you will do whatever is necessary to remove whatever gets in the way of love.

Determine how severe your immaturity is. Sometimes immaturity is a minor thing, like a wife withdrawing when she is upset. If so, simply making yourself aware of it may enable you to stop it. Sometimes immaturity is major, as when a spouse shuts down for days or weeks. In this case, the two of you may need to keep discussing it as a process, not as a one-time event.

It might be humbling to confront your own immaturity, but having a great marriage is worth the effort. Facing your immaturity is a mature thing to do—and it's the first step in overcoming it.

think about it | talk about it | live it

1 Which of the four indications of immaturity mentioned in this chapter do you see in yourself: detachment, control, irresponsibility, or self-centeredness? How have you demonstrated this trait (or these traits)?

2 How has your immaturity affected your marriage? How might dealing with your immaturity improve your relationship?

3 Read and meditate on 1 Corinthians 13:11 in the Bible. Jot down one or two vestiges of immaturity you intend to put behind you.

great marriage commitment 5

With God's help, I will identify and deal with my immaturity in order to preserve, help, and grow our love and connection.

simple secret 6

practice
humility

There's a humorous old country song that laments, "Lord, it's hard to be humble when you're perfect in every way." In reality, lack of humility in a marriage is no laughing matter. As you approach the sixth stop on your journey to a great marriage, it's time to get real with yourself about humility.

Humility doesn't get a good spin in our culture. But, properly understood, it really opens up things in a marriage. Basically, *humility is the capacity to experience the reality of who you are.* A humble person has no major illusions of self in either direction—good or bad, strong or weak.

Humility is important because it affects several main areas of love relationships.

What Humility Looks Like

Humility recognizes your need for your mate. When we toss aside our natural pride and self-sufficiency, underneath it is need for our mate. Rather than saying, "I don't know what I ever saw in him," a humble partner says, "We may not be doing well right now. But I know that I still need him, and I need our relationship. So I want to work on it." *Humility is the key to the resolution of not only conflicts in love but also the love relationship itself—* because love is about allowing the other person inside your head and your heart.

Humility accepts your inability to change or control your spouse. A great marriage flourishes only when both partners are free and have choices. When you are humble, you understand that you simply can't remove your partner's choice, no matter how much you would like him or her to see things your way. This does not mean that you cannot or should not influence your partner. You were designed to be a force for God, for love, and for growth with your partner. So be an influence. Say what you want and need. But be as protective of your mate's freedom as you are of your own.

Humility recognizes your own imperfections. Humble people don't pretend to be someone they are not. They admit and confess their weaknesses and failures to their partner. If you hide your bad parts or pretend they are not there, *you are not present in the relationship*. Humility ensures that you both "show up."

Humility allows you to show hurt without retaliating. When we act in humility, we don't give back what we receive; we give back better than we receive. As the apostle Paul once wrote: "Do not be overcome by evil, but overcome evil with good" (Romans 12:21). The best response to being hurt is not to retaliate, but to show your hurt to your partner. Tell him, for example, "When you dismissed my feelings about our sex life, it really hurt me." Or, tell her, "When you made fun of me at the party in front of our friends, it really hurt my feelings."

Humility brings about the best results because it doesn't play the fairness card. It plays the love and reality cards, which trump everything else in making a connection and building a great marriage.

How to Create Humility in Your Love Connection

Here are some ways to build good, healthy humility into your relationship so that you can keep your conflicts constructive:

Affirm that you do need each other, even in conflict. Practice saying these words out loud: "I need you, and I love you. Even when we are fighting, the need doesn't go away. And I want to resolve our conflicts so that it's easier to be safe with my need for you."

Reveal your fears to each other. Why have you been more proud and self-sufficient than humble in your relationship? Have you been afraid of rejection, being put down, being controlled, or being disrespected? Tell each other about these fears, and reassure each other that you don't want to be the cause of them.

Admit your flaws before your partner brings them up. One of the greatest signs of a healthy couple is that neither partner waits to be caught or confronted by an issue. He or she brings it up, so that the issue doesn't get in the way of love. So commit yourself to taking the first step: "Honey, I overspent. I screwed up. Let's deal with it." Or, "I got too mad at you over your staying at work too late again. That was my fault."

Celebrate humility and confront pride. Couples with humility have no tolerance for the false, arrogant, grandiose self. They confront it in each other and work on moving past it. At the same time, when one of you admits need, limitations, or faults, throw a party! Humility should draw you closer together and into the deeper aspects of each other's hearts and souls.

think about it | talk about it | live it

1 Do you struggle to acknowledge your need for your spouse?
  Why or why not?

2 Which of the four tips for creating humility in your relationship
  do you most need to work on? Identify one practical step you can
  take in the direction of exercising humility in your marriage.

3 Verbalize your love and need for your spouse today in a
  thoughtful and tangible way (a handwritten note or card,
  a small gift, a back rub).

great marriage commitment 6

*With God's help, I will resist pride and self-sufficiency in our relationship
and frequently express my love and need for you.*

simple secret 7

enjoy great sex by pursuing healthy sex

You might have been wondering since the

start of this journey, "When will we get to

the stuff about sex?" Well, here you go.

On the seventh day God rested, so in this

seventh chapter we invite you to take a break

from the heavy stuff to focus on the topic

of God's R&R for a great marriage.

Sex is the place that God has reserved for the unity of a marriage to be expressed in a unique and tangible way, by two bodies becoming "one flesh." In light of the high and honorable place that God has reserved for sex—and in light of the pleasure (and pain) it can bring—it is good to determine what healthy sex really is. You need to know, for it is an important part of preserving or re-establishing your love connection.

Healthy Sex Knows Best

First and foremost, healthy sex expresses *knowing one another in the deepest sort of intimacy, with the absence of fear, shame, hurt, or guilt.* Sex is where total vulnerability is expressed; it is a knowing of the other person's heart, mind, soul, and strength. Let's look at some of the things that help couples truly know each other in the deepest, most intimate ways.

Healthy sex is connected sex. Look up *intercourse* at www.webster.com, and here is what you find: (1) connection or dealings between persons or groups, (2) exchange, especially of thoughts or feelings, (3) physical sexual contact between individuals that involves the genitalia of at least one person.

If couples would just follow the dictionary, things would work out better for them: (1) deal with each other in a way that connects, (2) exchange thoughts and feelings, and (3) go for it!

Healthy sex is freely given. Healthy sex happens when both parties feel like they are there, in the act, by their own choosing. They have said yes with their bodies and their hearts. The problem comes when they say yes with their bodies and no with their hearts. The good and satisfying sexual relationship is one where neither women nor men are coerced—either to have sex when they don't want to or to do sexual acts they don't want to do.

Healthy sex is accepting sex. Good sex is not expert sex, but rather sex where both people feel accepted right where they are—and where the relationship feels okay right where it is—at whatever level of sexual health or competency it has. *Good sex is "failure-free" sex.* Give each other the freedom *to not get it right.*

Healthy sex is fun. Healthy sex is not only for deep communion but for fun and recreation as well. (You probably already knew that.) Healthy sex involves knowing all of each other—body, heart, mind, soul, and strength. Part of that is the physical act—the passion, desire, and coming together of two people as "one flesh."

Then there is "soul-level" sex that comes from your personality, feelings, interests, and expression of who you are in various ways that are unique to you and your mate. There is also sex that comes from connecting intellectually, with your minds and your beliefs coming together. But sometimes sex is just the physical hunger you have for one another. It may not be the deepest meeting of the hearts, but that's okay. Have fun, and get physical.

Healthy sex requires communicating. Couples with the greatest satisfaction are those who talk to each other about sex—about their wants, desires, likes, dislikes, fears, pains, insecurities, and whatever else comes into the picture. But opening up to each other requires safety. Create a space where you can connect *about* sex apart from connecting *through* sex. The goal is to know each other better, and to do that you need the safety to talk.

"Knowing" Each Other Is a Process

Sex means "to know" someone, and it takes time to know a person. Couples with healthy sex lives give each other time to get to know each other. They never assume they know everything about themselves or each other, and they are always learning. They allow the necessary time to be sure good things happen. If you invest time in growing together and keep working on your sex life, the returns will be worth it all.

1 What healthy-sex insights did you gain from the dictionary definition for *intercourse* quoted in this chapter?

2 Which of the five defining statements for healthy sex, listed under the heading "Healthy Sex Knows Best," is most helpful to you? Why?

3 We encourage you to add a "lab" session to this chapter. Set aside uninterrupted time to share your hearts and thoughts, enjoying the intimacy that may result.

great marriage commitment (7)

With God's help, I will try to know you better in every way so that our sexual relationship may become more fulfilling in every way.

simple secret 8

---

lavish
your partner
with grace

You're seven steps into the kind

of fulfilling marriage you've always wanted.

By now you have tasted some of the rewards,

and you have also discovered the kind of work

a great marriage takes. Don't pull back now.

This chapter will help bring the grace you need

to keep growing together.

Grace is undeserved favor. It is not an enhancement of your relationship; it is your very survival. Most of us don't realize how much grace we need in our marriages. We have an enormous empty place inside that only grace will fill. Life is hard, and love relationships take work. Every couple needs a big helping of grace to go deeper, reconnect, take risks, forgive, accept, be truthful, and help each other reach intimacy.

Couples who are aware of their deep need for grace are starting at the right place. *The need that both of you have for grace can draw you together emotionally, interpersonally, and spiritually.* You must come to the end of yourselves and admit to each other that you need each other's grace every day and in every way.

The Task and Privilege to Give Grace

Take on the task of being alert to your mate's need for grace. Though ultimately each partner is responsible for getting his or her needs met, the best couples are always concerned about meeting each other's needs. These two tips may help:

Be gracious in the content and tone of what you say. *Content* has to do with letting your spouse know, in words, that you care, the extent of how much you care, and what you value about him or her. For example: "I love you"; "My life is better because of you"; "I want us to be closer"; "I'm sorry I hurt you"; "I forgive you."

Tone is the way you speak. How you convey your words is as important as what you say. Your tone should be caring and warm, consistent with the grace you are providing.

Be a student of your partner. Grace is a universal need, but it should be administered in a highly individual and personal way. Observe your spouse and get to know him or her so that you can give the grace that's needed. This may be more work for men, because we are often not as acutely aware of all our spouse's characteristics. But becoming aware is worth the effort. What makes *her* happy? What scares her? What does she need to hear often? What does she dream of? Affirm and support her in these areas, and give her grace tailored to her life and ways.

Undeserved Means Undeserved

You and your partner qualify for each other's grace on a needs basis, not on a performance basis. That's true grace (Ephesians 2:8–9). Our natural tendency is to give love when our spouse acts lovingly toward us and to withhold love when he or she disconnects from us. This tendency puts your relationship under "the law"—a set of rules—and a law-based connection will never experience grace. One of the most connecting things couples learn is to provide grace even when one's partner has neither earned nor deserved it.

For example, when your mate has been hurtful and critical, you might say, "What you said really bothers me. Part of me wants to walk away right now. But I know we need to talk about this and get it straight. I don't want this to come between us." It is easy to do the opposite and protest, "I am the injured party here. It's your job to apologize and change." That stance will screw up your connection. Get out of the law orientation, and give your mate grace by taking the first step to move toward him or her. Be for your partner, be for the relationship, and face the issue so you can resolve it and move on with each other.

Get Grace

And when you can't find the grace inside you to give, get grace from outside yourself. God gives grace in your relationship with Him. Other people are also a major source of the grace we need for relationships, as we engage in "faithfully administering God's grace in its various forms" (1 Peter 4:10). Admitting our need and filling our emptiness from good sources is a far cry from our natural tendency to "try harder," "suck it up," and "commit more." It's much better to receive, experience, and lavish grace.

think about it | talk about it | live it

1 Find Ephesians 2:8–9 in your Bible and read these verses carefully. What similarities do you find between God's grace of salvation and the grace you should lavish on your spouse?

2 How would you rate your success at being gracious with your partner in both the content and tone of what you say? How might you improve in these areas?

3 Write a brief prayer asking God to fill you with His grace for your spouse. If your spouse also writes a prayer, take time together to offer both prayers aloud to God.

great marriage commitment 8

With God's help, I will strive to be a major provider of grace in your life through what I say and through meeting your unique needs.

simple secret 9

focus
on meeting
needs first

Still wondering if anything really significant

and lasting can be accomplished in your

marriage by learning twenty-one simple secrets?

Have some of the previous chapters stirred up

issues that have been difficult or even painful

to address? Hang in there. It's all part of

growing your marriage to greatness.

Some couples are derailed on their journey to a great marriage because they don't understand the difference between a need, a wish, and a preference. If partners fail to distinguish between what they really need and what they wish they had, they will either disconnect over issues that should not be connection-breakers, or they will put energy into the wrong things and thereby ignore the true needs that make a relationship thrive.

Needs, Wishes, and Preferences

What does one truly need in a marriage? *A true need is something that, if missing, results in damage.* For example, you need food, water, and shelter for physical survival. If these needs are not met, you could die. Similarly, we have basic relational needs that, if not met, can wreak havoc on a marriage.

Then there are those many things we wish for in marriage, but we don't truly need them. They might be essential to certain kinds of fulfillment, enjoyment, or quality of life, but we can live without them. Their absence doesn't damage our relationship. Preferences are like wishes. They have to do with the way we would ideally like things to be, but they are not always the way we find things to be.

Relationships truly have certain universal needs, and the first focus should be on those things. Wishes and preferences fall farther down the list. If you focus on the true needs of your relationship first, you can pursue those other areas of fulfillment as extra benefits, because you and your partner will have the kind of connection that enables both of you to grow to greater heights.

What Are Our True Needs?

Here are some of the basic, universal relational needs:

Emotional connection. Empathy, support, care, listening, understanding, and trust are all parts of what creates an emotional connection. It is the basic sense of being present with each other in a way that ends isolation, alienation, and aloneness.

Freedom. Love thrives only in an atmosphere of freedom. Where there is control, manipulation, or an inability to have an identity apart from the partner, love dies. You have a real need to set each other free from any and all kinds of control.

Forgiveness. All of us are sinners, and sin means we miss the mark of perfection. It's going to happen in every relationship—that's reality. If you punish each other for failure and do not forgive, your relationship will suffer damage and die.

Security. For love to grow, we need to know that our spouse's love is secure, unconditional, and forever. That is one of the biggest reasons the Bible calls for lifetime marriage. A commitment that preserves the connection through everything is essential.

Desiredness. From infancy, we need to know that we are desired by the people close to us—our family and close friends. Learn what causes your partner to feel desired, then act on what you learn.

Physical expression. Humans need to be touched, hugged, caressed, and nurtured physically. In addition, marriage needs a fulfilling sexual relationship. Like other aspects of touch, sex is intended to be respectful, mutual, accepting, desirous, secure, and free.

Time. No relationship ever perfectly met the needs of each person from the get-go. It takes time to develop love, to develop maturity, and to grow a relationship.

Keep the Important Things Important

Don't get caught up in fighting about your wishes. Work on those and try to fulfill as many as possible. But *do get caught up in focusing on your needs.*

Learn to communicate them, educate each other about them, stand up for them, nurture them, grow in your mutual ability to meet them, and do whatever you can to make sure they are being met.

Collectively, these needs are worth fighting *for*, not *about*. If you fight *about* these needs, you are probably violating one of them. But when you fight *for* them, you get closer to having them met.

think about it | talk about it | live it

1 Look again at the partial list of universal needs listed in this chapter. Which of your partner's needs do you feel you are adequately meeting? (If you're not sure, ask!) Which of your partner's needs do you need to invest more time and energy in meeting? (Again, if you're not sure, ask.)

2 What might you do to learn to better communicate your real needs to your partner?

3 Leave a written message for your partner to find today, completing the statement, "Thank you for meeting my need for . . ." Also consider leaving a small thank-you gift with the note.

great marriage commitment 9

With God's help, I will grow in my ability to discern and meet your real needs while striving also to fulfill your wishes and preferences.

simple secret 10

be
partners,
not
"dependents"

"I need you." "I'm incomplete without you."

"I can't make it without you." Sound like the

lyrics from love songs you've heard? Statements

like these make couples feel dependent on each

other, complete, and glad they aren't alone.

Dependency and love seem to merge as one.

But are they the same?

There is a world of difference between love and dependency, and that difference can have a big impact on your marriage. *Love* concerns itself with reaching out to another person, taking a stand for the benefits of that person. *Dependency* is a state of needing the other person in order to become complete and secure. It perceives the other as a need-meeting resource rather than a person in his or her own right, with a unique viewpoint and a set of needs.

In a healthy marriage, one person does not take primary responsibility for the other. That arrangement describes a parent-child relationship, and it's unhealthy in marriage. Rather, partners are to walk together as equals in life and growth. Each is still responsible for his or her own life and welfare.

Dependency in the Love Connection

Several problems can emerge in a relationship in which a partner's dependency has not been resolved:

Inability to love. True love is impossible when a person is dependent on his spouse. For example, a man's dependency might be so deep that he is more concerned about his survival than about his mate's. It makes for a one-sided relationship where love needs are not equally met.

Issues of separateness and difference. Dependent people do not enjoy the healthy differences of opinion, conflict, and arguments that help generate mutual love, respect, and learning. Any sense of separateness or difference makes a dependent partner feel abandoned and alone.

Power shifts. Often, the dependent person gives enormous power to the other partner, which affects the balance and mutuality of the relationship. Dependent partners abdicate control and decisions for the sake of avoiding difference and distance in the relationship. But this leads to greater problems.

Freedom problems. A dependent partner, for example, gets threatened by his or her spouse's expressions of freedom and perceives such choices as removing love and constancy.

Passion conflicts. Dependency creates problems with sex and romance, such as when a dependent husband is overly concerned with his needs, thus leaving his partner unfulfilled.

Growing Out of Dependency

Here are several keys to growing through dependency into secure and happy adult partners:

Find places for dependency to mature into self-sufficiency. Unresolved childhood dependency must be resolved. A good small group, support group, or counselor might be the answer. In this way, the person who struggles with dependency can find help and encouragement for becoming more complete, whole, and independent.

Encourage risk and autonomy. When, for instance, a dependent wife steps out on her own, affirm and support that decision. Allow her to speak her mind, confront, be angry, and do things without you, and let her know that you do not love her any less for doing so.

Confront the patterns. When one of you notices the warning signs of dependency, take action. In a gentle but direct way, say, "When you got jealous because I wanted a night out with the girls, I felt smothered. That's not good for either of us. Let's talk about how we can each enjoy healthy activities independent of each other."

Stay out of the comfort zone. There is comfortableness in dependency, because it tends to keep partners from disagreement or conflict. But you must stay out of this zone and address this tendency, because it can cause a relationship to become boring, unhealthy, stifling, and controlling.

Don't be afraid of need. At the same time, don't think that saying "I need you" is wrong or unhealthy. It's really good for you to need each other. You simply should understand what form of need you are referring to. Unhealthy dependency says, "I need you to survive, to be happy, to not be lonely, and to feel good about myself." But healthy and supportive dependency says, "I need you to be my loving partner, to be there for me as I will be for you, and to help me grow."

think about it | talk about it | live it

1 In what ways, if any, do you have an unhealthy dependency on people in general? On your spouse in particular?

2 If you recognize evidence of unhealthy dependency in yourself, what steps will you take to deal with it?

3 Compose a statement of healthy dependency to share with your spouse. Or, if you choose, compose one statement that represents your mutual (but healthy) dependency on each other.

great marriage commitment 10

With God's help, I will resist unhealthy dependency on you and help nurture a healthy, mutual dependency as equal partners.

simple secret **11**

---

cherish
your healthy
differences

You have reached the halfway point in your journey to a great marriage. Do you feel accomplished? Are you more confident and hopeful than when you began? Still skeptical or doubtful? You've come this far, so you might as well press on through the second half. We are confident that you will be glad you did.

Everyone has been around a couple so alike that they seem to be two sides of the same coin. Their interests, personalities, opinions, and even clothing styles are in sync. However, even "twinnish" partners differ from each other in some ways. That's the nature of individuality. Individuals are intricately designed and formed (Psalm 139:13–14). God created us to be different and unique, not cookie-cutter copies.

Immature love seeks sameness and similarity. That's why partners are often first attracted to each other by similar interests, likes, dislikes, and preferences. But as the relationship develops, mature love should supplant immature love. Instead of being threatened by your differences, you grow to enjoy them. Your life and perspective are enhanced and stretched by your partner's varying views and experiences.

Decidedly Different Strokes

Couples are different in a lot of ways. Here are just a few examples:

Feelers and thinkers. The feeler lives in emotion first and analyzes later, whereas the thinker lives in a world of logic. Often the feeler is perceived as childish and the thinker as grown-up. But feelers can also be mature, highly responsible adults who simply have an emotional nature.

Extroverts and introverts. The extrovert draws energy from being around people, while the introvert gravitates toward solitude and fewer social contacts.

Active types and reflective types. Some people are into aggression and initiative, such as preferring vacations of adventure, exploration, and risk. Others are quieter and would rather relax; they're more into enjoying free time in a hammock reading a novel.

Nurturing a great marriage includes encouraging, appreciating, and connecting with each other's differences. When you support the individual styles and preferences of your spouse, he or she will feel great value, love, and understanding from you.

Be aware of the tendency to make your own opinions and style a moral issue. There is no one "right way" between differences such as thinking and feeling. As a couple, do not tolerate moralizing of either style, but move toward accommodating them. Stay open, appreciative, and even protective of your partner's individuality.

Get Rid of Destructive Differences

Certain types of differences that are not just matters of style or preference are actually problems—and they cause negative things to happen in relationships. Destructive differences are not the same as stylistic differences. They come out of a person's brokenness, baggage from the past, immaturity, or character flaws. Healthy, growing couples will always have style differences, but they will have a minimum of destructive differences.

Here are several differences that are destructive in a marriage: detachment, irresponsibility, control, criticism and judgment, manipulation, self-centeredness, rage, guilt messages, deception, addictions, and violence.

And here are some ways to determine if a difference is destructive:

It cuts off love and trust. Destructive differences destroy intimacy. You cannot trust, feel safe with, or be totally vulnerable to someone who is not honest, dependable, and self-controlled.

It reduces freedom. Destructive differences don't leave the other partner free to make choices and speak the truth. A wife, for instance, might feel like she must walk on eggshells around her partner because she doesn't want to upset him "because he's an angry person; that's just who he is."

They are about "me," not "us." Destructive differences also tend to cause one partner to focus on dealing with "my problematic mate." A husband, for example, could find himself obsessing over his wife's "problems," trying to fix them—or having to protect himself from them.

If your marriage exhibits any of these behaviors, take action. Stand up to these destructive differences. Tell your partner that you won't tolerate how they affect the relationship. It is a good sign if he or she becomes concerned about them and wants to work on them, for there is a lot of help available, such as small groups, healthy spiritual growth contexts and churches, and therapy. And the problem is quite fixable; so don't give up, but ally with your mate in treating the destructive differences.

think about it | talk about it | live it

1 Name two or three healthy differences between you and your
   spouse. In what ways do these differences enhance your relationship?

2 What potentially destructive differences, if any, do you see in
   your relationship?

3 List one or two ways you can encourage your healthy differences,
   and one or two ways you can discourage or eliminate any
   destructive differences.

great marriage commitment 11

*With God's help, I will celebrate and encourage the healthy ways in which we are
different, and I commit to confront destructive differences that may arise.*

simple secret 12

share
your
feelings

"How was I supposed to know you didn't want

to go?" one of you says, referring to the other's

resentment toward going to the in-laws'

for the holidays. Uh-oh. Some feelings didn't

get communicated, and somebody's feelings

got hurt. Today we want to show you how

to keep this from happening.

Sometimes partners slowly stop communicating what they really think and feel, and they get further and further away from each other emotionally. And when hidden feelings are ultimately revealed, it is often too late. Let's examine several reasons why the sharing stops in the first place and how detachment occurs in a relationship.

Sharing is not safe. Many couples find that defensiveness, attack, blame, judgment, pulling away, anger, and other bad things happen in their relationship when they share what is in their hearts. They don't feel safe, so they stop sharing.

Old fears keep them from sharing. For some couples, the things they bring into the marriage keep them from sharing. They carry fears from past experiences that have taught them that sharing your heart could lead to abandonment, criticism, rejection, abuse, disapproval, anger, escalation, breakdown in connection, withdrawal, attack, or judgment. So they hold back, and intimacy suffers.

They lack skills or know-how. Some people did not grow up in families that communicated well, and they didn't learn what real, honest communication looks like. They are able to share with their partner when there is little threat or difficulty. But when feelings run high and issues are tough, they just don't know how to share their heart.

They think their desires or wants are unimportant. Many people have been taught that their wants don't matter, are selfish, or have little or no chance of being fulfilled. So they shut down from feeling those things and communicating them.

Whatever your reason, hiding your feelings through lies and miscommunication is not only dishonest, but it can also damage your marriage. You must learn to own and to share your feelings.

Tips for Emotional Honesty

Opening up your hearts together is what intimacy is all about. Here are some tips on how to re-establish your connection:

Stop fudging. Most people don't lie outright; they just fudge the truth a little to keep the peace. It sounds like this: "Whatever you want is okay"; "No, I'm not angry"; "It didn't bother me at all." Honesty means not sugarcoating the truth but telling it as it is.

Be direct. Don't beat around the bush; communicate directly. Learn to say: "I want . . . "; "I feel . . . "; "I think . . . "; "I don't like it when . . ."; "I prefer . . . " and so on. "I" statements draw your partner in. They are direct expressions from the heart.

Face your fears. If you are not direct and honest about your feelings, you are probably afraid of something, perhaps even your spouse. Face your fears and be truthful with your partner. When you do, you might find that you have solved the problem and that your mate is much more able to handle the truth than you realized.

Say more with less. One woman I (Henry) counseled was having trouble connecting with her boyfriend, causing him to stall in committing to her. I gave her an assignment I like to give to many people: "Say whatever you want to say in one-third the number of words." She was beating around the bush, getting so lost in words that what she really wanted to say was lost. She tried it, and they ended up married and happy.

Let your mate have his or her own reaction. You cannot control your mate's reaction to what you share, and you are not responsible for it. Intimacy comes from the risk of telling the truth and allowing your mate to respond accordingly.

Address the reasons you can't talk. Look for things that are making honesty difficult, like judgmentalism, defensiveness, contempt, disgust, shaming, anger, reactivity, shutdowns, or blame. Address ways that the two of you respond. Begin with the question, "What do I do to make it hard for you to be honest with me?"

Make the problem the problem, not your partner. Most disconnects could be prevented if couples would just learn one principle: talk about the issue instead of smearing your partner's character and personhood. For example, when your partner is unexpectedly late, don't say, "You're so selfish and irresponsible." A more honest, direct approach is, "I need you to call me when you are going to be late." Addressing a specific problem, without slamming your partner in the process, conveys helpful information to solve the problem.

think about it | talk about it | live it

1 When has your mate been surprised by your feelings—when you thought you were communicating them clearly? When have you been similarly surprised by your mate?

2 Can you personally identify with one or more of the reasons why people hide their feelings, as stated in this chapter? Explain and give an example.

3 Which of the tips for emotional honesty do you most need to put into practice? How will you do that?

great marriage commitment 12

With God's help, I will improve my skill at sharing my feelings openly and honestly with you.

simple secret 13

curb the
communication
stoppers

We belive Secret 13 can be lucky for you in the area of improving your conversation and connection as partners. As you read on, you'll gain some practical tips on improving your communtication and your marriage.

As partners grow in their skill at communicating, it's like they are building a bridge for the sharing of their deep hearts and lives with each other. The problem is that many of what we call "communication stoppers" can dynamite that bridge, leaving partners angry, hurt, distanced, and alone. While no one ever communicates perfectly, some do it much worse than others. They perpetually say things that don't help; in fact, what they say makes things even worse. Many do it without realizing what they're doing, and certainly without realizing there is a better way. But there is.

Find and Fix Your Communication Stoppers

The list below is a guide for what not to do when trying to connect with your mate. Learn them well—and learn to catch yourself before you do them. If you can avoid these twelve communication stoppers, you will be way ahead in the journey toward building a lasting bridge between you and your partner.

1. Don't devalue what your mate says. No matter what you think of it, when your mate says something, take it seriously. Treat your partner with respect. Really listen—don't just hear the words.

2. Don't minimize. When your spouse feels something strongly or thinks something is significant, you must connect with that feeling and not try to shut it down by saying something like, "It's not that bad," or "Oh, that's so ridiculous!"

3. Don't get defensive. Defensiveness is when you try to fight off anything that makes you feel bad. Your defensive anger, pouting, excuses, justifications, and similar moves all serve to shut down your partner. So listen to your partner, take in what he or she says, and embrace it. Doing so shows that you love your mate.

4. Don't criticize or put down your mate. Complaints voiced in a critical spirit do not solve problems like constructive feedback does. Criticism puts the other person down and makes him or her feel bad. So say what must be said in a way that is not a put-down or character assassination.

5. Don't overreact or escalate. The more emotional a topic is, the more reactive and defensive we tend to get. Some people shut down, retreat, or fight, while others tend to lose connection, rationality, and good judgment. Learn to recognize your reaction pattern, and when it happens, take a time-out until you calm down.

6. Avoid shutdown statements and behaviors. Shutdown statements are things you say when you are mad, hurt, or overwhelmed. These statements totally stop communication. Here are some examples: "Fine!" (when it's not fine); "Nothing!" (when it's something); "It doesn't matter!" (when it does). Other examples include the silent treatment or walking away.

7. Don't shift the blame. Shifting the blame means trying to explain away responsibility for your own behavior as being caused by your mate's behavior. Responding to feedback with counteraccusation always dynamites an interpersonal connection.

8. Avoid sarcasm. Sarcasm communicates disdain and lack of respect, closing down hearts and turning things in the wrong direction.

9. Avoid extremes and global statements. Such statements ("you always," "you never") are neither true nor helpful. They just leave the other person judged and feeling bad.

10. Don't immediately jump to your perspective. Healthy conversation is a give-and-take. But some people do not connect because they take a comment as the signal to talk about their side of things only. The other person is left hanging.

11. Don't try to fix it. Most of the time, a problem that involves feelings

can't be fixed until the feelings are heard and understood. Other times, the problem doesn't need to be fixed, just heard and understood.

12. Don't go "all bad." Some people go "all bad" when they take feedback as criticism, then defend themselves by playing the victim. The expression of a need by one partner launches the other into a sad diatribe: "I can't please you no matter what I do. Nothing I do is good enough. I'm just a bad spouse."

Enlist each other's help in watching for these twelve communication stoppers. Make it a project. Devise a signal, if necessary, by which one can tell the other when communication is breaking down.

think about it | talk about it | live it

1 When you hear the term *shutdown*, what recent interactions or communication patterns come to mind?

2 Which of the twelve communication stoppers do you most need to work on? What's your plan of action? Be specific.

3 Find and read these verses in your Bible: Proverbs 18:13 and Proverbs 20:5. Summarize in writing what these verses say to you personally.

great marriage commitment 13

With God's help, I will consciously eliminate the communication stoppers I use, in order to help build a strong bridge of connection between us.

simple secret 14

draw out
your partner's
Heart

Now you are two-thirds of the way

on your journey to a great marriage.

You're really accomplishing something

of lasting value. Keep investing in each

other. Keep talking deeply and praying

fervently with each other. And keep putting

into practice these daily principles.

You won't regret it!

One of the most powerful keys to an intimate and passionate marriage is also one of the most unnatural and counterintuitive things you will ever do. It is called *validation*, and it refers to your ability to understand and empathize with the feelings and experiences of your mate, *especially when your view is not the same as his or hers.*

Validation is even more important when your mate sees something negative in your behavior—something you don't see as negative. For instance, if a wife wants to validate her husband, she needs to draw him out and help him feel that she truly hears him on a deep level. She should let him know that she really understands his feelings. Proverbs 20:5 says, "The purposes of a man's heart are deep waters, but a man of understanding draws them out." As husbands and wives express their hearts and strive for understanding, they are drawing each other out.

Why Validation?

Validation is necessary in relationships because we all need to be heard and understood. We don't move forward to resolve conflicts when we feel misunderstood.

Think about the last fight you had with your partner. When you were trying to get your feelings across, did your partner minimize, dismiss, or simply not understand what you were saying? What was that like for you? How did that affect your ability and desire to hear his or her side of things? Most likely, not receiving validation from your mate disconnected things even more.

When couples learn to validate each other's experiences, they feel that their partner is part of their life again. They no longer feel alone.

Think about those occasions when you've made the common mistake of joking about the wrong thing at the wrong time, hurting your mate's feelings in front of friends or family. Validation would sound something like, "I'm really sorry, honey. That must have been awkward for you." The essential element is that you are trying to understand what the experience was like from your partner's perspective.

Validation has nothing to do with whether you agree or disagree with your partner. Validating your mate's feelings as being important and real does not mean you accept his or her view as truth and reality. A viewpoint is one thing; reality is another, and they need to be dealt with separately. Validation comes first, and *then* reality. People are much more open to hearing the facts after their viewpoint has been validated.

The Work of Validation

Validation is unnatural; it takes work. Here we will list for you the kind of work that will help you and your partner validate one another:

Get out of the way. Learn to suspend your own point of view, to put your way of seeing things aside in order to leave room for your partner's feelings and experiences. Give up the attempt to be seen as good, innocent, or right, and be willing to endure some angry feelings from your mate without responding to them in kind.

Empathize first. When you know your partner is upset, angry, or hurt, think first about understanding how he or she is feeling and why. Don't make the mistake of insisting on being heard, instead of really hearing your partner. Empathy must go both ways.

Ask, don't answer. When you validate your mate, seek information about his or her experience. Get to the pain and emotions. Don't try to provide answers or "fixes." That can come later. Instead of saying, "Well, you'll feel better if you . . . " say, "That sounds awful; tell me more." You are building a strong, adaptable, and safe bridge with your spouse, not only for resolving this conflict, but future conflicts as well.

Check it out. When your partner explains a viewpoint, ask if you are understanding his or her experience. This way, your mate can guide you and let you know if you are way off base. And even if you are, he or she is likely to appreciate that you are making a real effort to connect with his or her experience and perspective.

Live with the tension of unhappiness. We tend to want a happy ending, and quickly, especially when our partner is upset with us. Couples who love well and deeply learn to "sit" with the unhappy feelings of their partners. Feelings take time to resolve, and they cannot be rushed. Be patient, present, and empathetic. Your mate's unhappy feelings won't last. Stay for the long haul.

think about it | talk about it | live it

1 Is your partner receiving validation from you? Give supporting evidence from a recent disagreement or fight.

2 What keeps you from freely and consistently giving your spouse the gift of simply being heard and understood? How will you remove that hindrance?

3 Finish the following statement in writing: *When I sense that you are really listening and trying to understand my experiences and feelings, it makes me feel. . . .* Take time today to read your completed statements to each other.

great marriage commitment 14

With God's help, I will seek to improve my ability to validate your feelings and experiences, even when I don't agree with them.

simple secret 15

take sex
beyond
the bedroom

Here's another strategically placed principle

in your journey, which will help keep

the heavy topics in balance. Take some time

today to focus on the joys and pleasures

of your sexual life, especially how it can pervade

your other daily and weekly experiences.

The music plays in the background; the moon glistens above. The lovers gaze at each other on the balcony as the reflection of city lights shine pathways to heaven. The man and woman caress each other, and then he leads her through the open glass door, the draperies gently blowing in the wind. The lights fade, and the lovers disappear into the depths of romantic and sexual bliss, leaving the audience to fill in the blanks. . . .

Hollywood depictions of sex are engaging to watch, but they lead many couples to expect that all they need for a fulfilling sexual relationship is moonlight, a soft breeze, and the right background music. The movies never show the couple five years later, fifty-hour workweeks busier, forty pounds heavier, or any of the other eventualities that make for real life. In reality, sustaining a sexual connection in your marriage takes focus, attention, and work—but the effort is worth it in the end.

Keep the Home Fires Burning

Today we will give you several more tips on how to keep your sex life alive and healthy:

Talk, talk, talk. We simply cannot overemphasize how important talking is to your sexual connection. You must talk to each other about things, like how you feel about your sex life and how you would like it to be different; how you feel about foreplay and how you would like it to be different; what your mate does that you really like and don't like; what positions you like, don't like, or would like to try; your fears about sex; what makes you feel tense and relaxed during sex; and what attitudes, actions, and words help you feel safer and more fulfilled.

Have nonsexual sensual exercises. One of the most important things that sex therapists have couples do is nongenital pleasuring exercises—sometimes referred to as sensate focus. The idea is to pleasure your mate through full-body touch, massage, stroking, caressing, and so on. Sensate focus helps you find out what feels good, emotional, erotic, relaxing, intimate, connecting, and so on. It helps partners rediscover—or discover for the first time—the broader range of their sexuality.

Kill evaluation. There are few bigger desire- and performance-killers than evaluation and performance anxiety. What is going on inside your head as you are making love? Are you wondering if your mate thinks you're a good lover, if you're not sexy or too fat, if your partner is enjoying what you're doing, if you're saying enough or too much, and so on? Stop evaluating and start experiencing. Get into the moment and feel it. Focus on it. Talk about it, but don't judge. Judging leads only to fear and shame.

Sex begins long before "sex." Sex does not begin when you begin "sex." It is an outgrowth of the connection, love, and tenderness that you have shown up to that moment. For example, men, pursue your mate in nonsexual ways throughout the day. And pursue all aspects of her, not just her body. Be loving, kind, tender, proactive, and helpful. Chances are she'll make you glad you did.

Eliminate pressure. Get performance pressure out of your bedroom—and out of your relationship. Don't put pressure on your spouse to be aroused or satisfied, or to arouse or satisfy you, within a certain time or with certain behaviors. The bottom line here is that sex is about a relaxed, emotional, loving, relational, and physical response. You are a team to pleasure each other, not to perform for each other or judge each other or even judge yourselves.

Get physical. Research shows that people in better physical condition have better sex. Get in shape, and eat a healthful diet. Get more rest, and reduce stress. All these disciplines have been shown to improve sex.

Make time to make love. Loving takes time and space. If you are doing it as an afterthought—with whatever few minutes and little energy left at the end of the day—then that will be the quality of your love life. Be more proactive. Schedule time for sex. Vary it. Go on overnighters. Have sex appointments. Create protected time for making love.

Support each other. When either of you has a struggle of any kind or needs to grow in some way, support each other. When one of you is challenged, hurting, or under stress, both of you struggle. Stay close to each other during those times and bring each other along. Loyally supporting and accepting each other when either of you struggles is a move toward better lovemaking.

think about it | talk about it | live it

1   Select one or two tips you most need to work on to help improve your sex life. How will you implement these tips to bring greater satisfaction to your mate?

2   Take the initiative to schedule an intimate encounter for you and your spouse at a time and place that works for both of you. Write an alluring, creative invitation to the encounter and deliver it to your spouse. Include in the invitation a request that your spouse provide a "menu" of pleasures he or she would enjoy. Plan the encounter for your mate's enjoyment.

great marriage commitment 15

With God's help, I will seek to broaden and enrich our sex life by nurturing our intimacy beyond merely the physical act.

simple secret 16

nudge
each other
to be more
than
you are

Do you realize that your spouse

is your greatest asset to personal growth

and success on this journey to marriage

greatness? It's true. Simple Secret 16

will alert you and equip you to take best

advantage of God's choice instrument

of growth in your life.

We all need nudges in our marriages. Nudges ensure that each of us can be more than we are, and they're a way to help each other on that path. They have to do with our expectations of each other. *You are to love each other enough to expect your partner to grow into more than he or she is right now.*

Nudges Are Okay

You want your partner to be a better person—more loving, responsible, real, spiritual, and honest. You want him or her to connect to you better. You want a mate free of bad habits and addictions. Your love drives you to desire these things. They are good wishes for your partner's best. They are also for your best and for the reconnection and depth of your intimacy.

Having higher expectations does not mean that you don't accept your mate as is. No one grows or truly changes from the heart unless he or she is first accepted *right now*. There is really no conflict between acceptance and expectations. In fact, they are partners in intimacy.

Sometimes, one partner will think the other is being critical or unaccepting because of various standards, requirements, and expectations. A husband, for example, might say, "If you love me, love me as I am." The answer to that is, "I do love you as you are. But if I didn't want you to be more than you are, I would not really be loving you." When you have high (yet reasonable) standards, you are defining what you want and need. You are establishing a healthy structure for love to grow.

Why You Need Expectations

You need love in your marriage, lots of it, but you also need to be honest, to confront, and to have expectations of each other. Here are some reasons:

Expectations get you out of the comfort zone. When two people become committed to each other, they almost always start regressing into comfortable and nongrowing patterns. They might stop working out and start gaining weight. The home gets a little sloppy. They stop listening to each other the way they used to and get into their own separate worlds. This regressive pattern leads one to rationalize, *I have my love and this person accepts me, so I'll just be me.* If you begin to think this way, you've fallen into the comfort zone.

When this happens, spouses should grant mutual permission to nudge one another out of the comfort zone. When expectations and requirements are given lovingly and not harshly, they are healthy and effective.

Expectations help you see your blind spots. We are often unaware of when we aren't at our best. Who is better than your mate at identifying something you are doing to hinder your growth, development, and success? For example, your partner may lovingly address your tendency toward complacency with, "I want you to push more, take some risks, and stop being satisfied with the average."

Expectations help you and your partner grow together. Partners who encourage each other to be all that they can be tend to be closer, more romantic, and more interested in each other. If you are growing personally, emotionally, and spiritually, your heart is being enlarged. You are learning to give and receive love. And that translates into a direct benefit for connection.

Where to Start

Here are some things you can do to "nudge" your love life along:

Walk out of the comfort zone. Talk about how the two of you want to be safe, accepting, and unconditional in your love. But at the same time, humbly submit to each other in growth areas and problems. With grace, love, and healthy expectations, couples become better individuals and better lovers.

Become a team. Work together on what each of you wants for yourself and your mate. Be a partner, an encourager, and a coach to each other. Make personal growth and improvement something for the two of you.

Celebrate change. When one of you makes a few moves in the right direction, celebrate it! Change is not easy. It takes time to deal with stagnation and sameness. When your partner makes the effort and takes the risk, even a small one, affirm and reinforce him or her.

think about it | talk about it | live it

1 Is your spouse in a comfort zone that is stifling personal growth and the growth of your marriage? Describe it.

2 Ask your spouse if you are in such a comfort zone. Prepare to welcome his or her nudge, not feel threatened by it.

3 What healthy and loving expectations do you have for your spouse? Jot down a few specifics. How will you nudge your partner forward while still demonstrating your complete acceptance?

great marriage commitment 16

With God's help, I will engage in and welcome healthy, balanced nudging to promote growth individually and as a couple.

simple secret 17

deal
with Hurt
as it
happens

The last five phases of this journey are aimed

at helping you deal with conflict in your marriage.

You know that everyone is quite capable of

unleashing cutting words and freezing out

his or her partner with the silent treatment.

Implementing these tips won't make

your marriage perfect, but it will help

lift your marriage to greatness.

Sometimes in my marriage seminars, I (Henry) ask couples to turn to each other and say, "I promise that I will hurt you." They usually look stunned. Then I explain, "That wonderful person whom you love so much and desire to be with is an imperfect person and will do things to hurt you. As wonderful as he or she is, your spouse will fail you at times, and it's going to hurt."

Great marriages are not ones in which there is no pain, but in which pain is accepted as part of the package. As a result, the couple consciously focuses on getting better at processing pain and resolving conflict.

False Expectations

Many people never find the wonder and joy that marriage *can* provide because they look for something it can't provide. People set themselves up for failure by expecting a good marriage to be one without pain, and that expectation comes in at least three forms:

The wish for a childhood fantasy. Many people enter adulthood with the childish dream of marrying a fantasy prince or princess who will always make life fun and happy—and who would never hurt them. So when those hurts do come and the marriage is not fun anymore, many cut and run. Only when couples set aside childhood fantasies about marriage can they find the pleasure of genuine adult love.

The wish for a pain-free life. We live in a fallen world, and bad things happen. As Jesus said, "In this world you will have trouble" (John 16:33). In a good relationship, partners not only face the reality that they will hurt each other, but they face and process the general pain of life together.

The wish to make up for past hurt. When the past has held substantial hurt and pain, a person may dream of a relationship that will one day make it all better. But even when he or she finds a healthy relationship with a good person, disappointment is still going to be part of the package.

This leads to double hurt—the hurt itself plus the greater hurt of being disappointed that the longed-for "rescue" did not happen.

The Reality

Partners in great marriages develop the following attitudes and practices that preserve the connection, even when one has hurt the other:

Accept the fact that your mate will sometimes do things that hurt you. When you accept this fact, you will be able to deal with the hurts when they come, and those hurts won't destroy the connection and love you share.

Hang on to the things you love about your mate, even when he or she disappoints you. Do not label your mate as "all bad." Don't let the hurt blind you to all of those good qualities.

When hurt happens, face it with honesty and directness. Great marriages do not deny problems—they face them. When you are hurt, tell each other.

But speak the truth in love, not anger (Ephesians 4:25–26).

When you are the one who has hurt the other, apologize. Confess your wrongdoing—don't excuse it!—and empathize with the hurt you have caused. The worst thing you can do is rationalize it or explain it away. Confess your offense, and ask forgiveness.

When you are hurt, grieve it, and then forgive. Forgiveness is as vital as your digestive tract. It is the way we metabolize and remove waste from the system of a relationship. We'll talk more about forgiveness in Chapter 21.

If the hurt is severe, get support and healing, and process the pain. If a major hurt had been inflicted, grieving the hurt and letting it go may be impossible without outside help.

Get straight about what is worth being hurt over. Some things are not worth bringing up or making into an issue. One of the most annoying things in life is being around someone who is annoyed by everything. If you find yourself hurt continually by much of what your mate does, you may need outside help to correct your perspective.

Work together on how you process pain and hurt. Talk to each other about how to let each other know when you are hurt. Discuss what you need from each other in those moments. See resolving hurt and conflict as one of the most important skills you can develop.

think about it | talk about it | live it

1 Did you enter marriage with one of the false expectations mentioned in this chapter? If so, describe it and how it affected your relationship.

2 What action steps, if any, do you think might be good for you to take in light of the insights in this chapter? List them and how you intend to get started.

great marriage commitment 17

With God's help, I will grow to better accept the inevitability of hurt in our relationship and apply myself to deal with hurt as it happens.

simple secret 18

fight
for win-win
solutions

Has your daily journey toward a great marriage sparked any good fights yet? You might ask, "Isn't 'good fight' an oxymoron?" We're here to tell you that good fights and healthy arguments are vital to the marriage you're after.

Bruce and Kris looked at each other in amazement. "We did it!" Kris exclaimed, then they high-fived each other. Their first successful fight. They had argued over an issue, resolved it, and still felt connected to each other. It was a great step in their marriage.

Couples who know how to fight right will love right. Healthy arguments are an important part of connection, reconnection, and passion. After all, at its healthy core, fighting is about love. It is an attempt to resolve differences so that love can return and grow.

There are many kinds of fights. Some are about preferences (movies and restaurants). Some are about values (honesty and faithfulness). Some are about communication ("I never said you looked fat in that dress."). Some are about our own issues (such as baggage from the past). No matter what sparks the fight, you need a way to address these and any other disagreements you might have.

Keep the Goal in Mind

Couples who fight well keep the goal in mind: connection. It's all about your love life and about the relationship. It's not about fixing, being right, or proving someone wrong. *What is important is not the problem; it is how the problem affects the relationship.* If it distances the two of you, it works against the connection.

This fact is easy to miss in the heat of the argument. Fighting can bring out the worst in us, and it can easily escalate to power plays and revenge. But you must begin and end with the goal in mind: *This is about our relationship. This is about building a better connection.*

Rules for a Fair and Fruitful Fight

Be direct and specific. Indirect charges sound like this: "You do the wrong things and don't do the right things." Specific charges sound like this: "I don't think you are doing your share with the kids after work," or "When you spend hours on the computer, I feel really alone and disconnected from you." When you are direct, you give your partner someone to talk to and something specific to talk about. Being indirect and evasive causes distance and anxiety because your partner has nowhere to go with his or her issues. When you are specific, your partner knows exactly what you are seeing as the problem and what steps might be required to change things.

Keep it two-way. Good fighting is a dialogue between two people. Don't get caught in thinking that if you say your piece, it's all done. Your partner needs equal time. If you fail to make it a conversation, you'll end up with alienation or escalation.

Have a structure. Many fights seem to be the same fight over and over, signaling that the issue has not been resolved. Resolving it for good will require some structure. Here are four suggestions:

1. Somebody be the traffic cop. When a discussion involves a lot of diverting, missing the point, blaming, and defensiveness, one of you needs to step up and stop the flow. It may sound like this: "We're losing focus here. Let's get back to the main point."

2. Set time limits. If the discussion is not moving forward, set a time limit. It will help you stay focused and more mindful that you have a goal to reach.

3. Agree beforehand that escalation isn't okay and won't be tolerated. You might say something like, "If you go beyond normal anger to yelling and cursing at me, I will end this and walk out. We'll have to finish it later."

4. Don't avoid all anger. Relationships have passion, and anger is part of passion. But pay attention to the degree and tone of anger. The degree should not be so great that it distances or scares your partner. Anger should also be "clean," not sarcastic, vengeful, or guilt inducing. When the issue is dealt with, the anger it sparked should go away.

Normalize fighting. Normalize your arguments by taking the fear and power out of them. Couples who become anxious or avoidant about fighting will either not solve their problems or have enormous blowups when they do argue. It is not uncommon for couples in love to have some sort of disagreement every day, ranging from being on time for dinner to how much someone spent. These disagreements don't have to be a big deal, but they will be if you try to avoid them.

When you and your partner fight, talk about it in the "now": "Look, I know we're both mad right now, but I want you to know that I love you and want us to be safe with each other." This approach helps integrate love, truth, reality, and passion into the connection.

think about it | talk about it | live it

1 What are most of your conflicts and disagreements with your spouse about—preferences, values, communication, or personal issues? Give an example.

2 Which of the rules for fair and fruitful fighting have you overlooked in conflict resolution with your partner? What has been the result of these oversights?

3 Write a brief "love note" to your spouse on the topic of your arguments and fights.

great marriage commitment 18

With God's help, I will argue and fight with you in a fair and loving way, with the goal of deepening our connection.

simple secret 19

---

exercise
trust

Did you notice that you have only

a few pages left in this book? And look

how much ground you have already covered.

You're driving toward the finish line,

so don't let up now. The prize is the great

marriage you and your mate both desire.

Trust is *the ability to be totally real, authentic, and unguarded with your partner.* It means being able to bring all parts of you to your mate, good and bad, strong and weak, without fear of condemnation or judgment. It has to do with not needing to edit or color what you say or who you are, for fear of a negative reaction.

In the Hebrew Scriptures, there is a word for *trust* (*batach*) that conveys the idea of "carelessness" (Psalm 22:9). In other words, when you trust someone, you aren't paranoid about what you say or do. You let things slip sometimes, and even if that causes a problem, it's a little problem, not a catastrophe. Who wouldn't want to have a connection with one's partner that was characterized by the ability to be "careless" in this way?

Think about the last time you opened up to your partner about a failure or fear. When you were open and vulnerable, did he or she move toward you, make it safe for you, and draw you out? Or did your mate move away, become critical, or even dismiss the issue? This is not meant to be an indictment of partners. It is simply a way for you, as a couple, to begin to evaluate the level of trust the two of you have in each other.

Couples who have learned how to trust receive many benefits in return. They are able to connect at deeper levels. They desire to be with each other and want to give to each other in gratitude. They are able to have more passion, as passion can emerge only in a safe and trusting context. Trust forms the foundation of the love life you desire.

Three Elements of Trust

Couples can work on trust and improve it. Let's look at three primary elements that, when present in the relationship, create an atmosphere of trust and safety:

Risk. No risk, no trust. To develop trust, you need to extend yourselves beyond your comfort zones and take a risk. Risk in a relationship involves exposing vulnerable parts of yourself to your partner. You need to share your thoughts, feelings, and experiences—including the ones that are negative, painful, or fragile. This might include fears, hurts, mistakes, sins, and aspects of yourself that you are ashamed of or you wish weren't there.

How do you think your partner will respond to your openness? Whatever it might be, you need to take the risk anyway because *you are designed to bring every part of your being into the relationship.* God made you to connect on all levels. Couples who can navigate risk well are on their way to the benefits of trust.

Here are some "risky" things partners sometimes need to say:

- "I'm afraid that you will see all my flaws and disconnect from me."
- "I sometimes pretend that I'm okay when I am not."
- "I don't know how to be who you need me to be."

- "I can be really selfish and demanding with you."

- "I have a bad habit that I've been keeping from you."

- "I spent the money in a way that I had agreed not to."

Welcome. Appreciate your partner's effort and humility in doing something uncomfortable for the sake of the relationship. Extend grace and love with no hint of condemnation. You do not have to agree with what your partner says or does to be welcoming. The best way to understand the concept is that you are welcoming your partner's vulnerability, not necessarily the right or wrong of what he or she is saying. Think about how hard it is for you to take the risk with your partner, and give him or her the same grace you need.

Trustworthiness. Trustworthiness means that you take your partner's investment in you very seriously and that you will not do anything to break the trust between you. Trustworthiness requires time; it can be proven only over a series of experiences. A trustworthy couple puts a high value on faithfulness, loyalty, and reliability.

Here are a few examples of being trustworthy:

• Maintaining your welcome for your partner as a constant thing.

• Never using against your partner anything he or she shares with you.

• Keeping your promises and commitments.

• Saying no to any form of deceptive talk or lies, large or small.

• Owning up when you make mistakes and changing what needs to be changed.

Without risk, you will never know if you can trust your mate. Without welcome, you will simply detach or pretend. Without trustworthiness, you will not believe the welcome is real. Make all three a covenant in your connection with each other.

think about it | talk about it | live it

1 How would you rate your success at building the three elements of trust (risk, welcome, and trustworthiness) into your marriage relationship?

2 Why is it a gift to have a spouse who keeps no secrets from you? What, if anything, is keeping you from giving that gift to your mate?

3 Jot down one or two things you have not yet risked sharing with your spouse. Determine the best time to share these things, then share them.

great marriage commitment (19)

With God's help, I will grow in trusting and being open to you while welcoming and cherishing your trust and openness.

simple secret 20

welcome rules when needed

*The finish line is just ahead, but don't
ease up quite yet. Give these last two sessions
your best effort. It will bless you and your
partner well beyond your expectations!*

Reflect for a minute on your first date with your partner. Remember where you were, what you did, how you felt, and how you experienced him or her? At any point during that event did you discuss what kind of rules and structures you should put in place in order to get to know each other?

No way! People don't become interested in each other and fall in love because they are into rules. The relationship starts with attraction, love, excitement, and passion. Rules are the farthest thing from their minds.

However, as time moves on, many couples have found that they can be forgetful, hurtful, and selfish with each other. Trust and understanding can be somewhat fragile and easily bruised. So when one partner hurts the heart of the other, it sets the entire relationship back many steps.

This is where relational rules and structure come into your love life. There are times when they are necessary to treat a wound. Like a cast on a broken limb, relational rules can preserve, protect, and even repair the love between partners.

Imposing rules and structure applies to a host of problems, large and small—emotional unavailability, control, irresponsibility, defensiveness, chronic tardiness, overspending, unfaithfulness, and rage. These behaviors—and others as well—can bruise love and trust. They must be dealt with.

Not the Ideal, but the Real

Just as broken limbs aren't ideal, neither is having lots of rules for your relationship. If you and your partner have made responsibility, care, sacrifice, and freedom parts of your normal behavior with each other, you don't need lots of rules. You can trust your partner to act in your best interest, and you can rest in that.

For example, if your husband is romantically faithful, how often do you say, "I want you to make sure you're behaving appropriately with the women you meet at work"? Probably never. You don't need that rule because he lives that rule. But suppose he flirts or has a history of unfaithfulness. This is a real problem for you, then, and it should be addressed. You might have to establish some sort of accountability with him until he proves himself trustworthy, such as being able to reach him at any time and requiring that he tells you who he is with.

Think of rules as protection that protects and preserves. Use them when needed, but use as few of them as possible, so that freedom and love can flourish as much as possible.

When Do We Need Rules?

When do you need rules? Here are two criteria:

1. One of you is hurting the other and causing alienation and distance.
2. Appeals to the offender aren't working.

Ideally, when one person is harsh or hurtful, the partner says something like, "What you just said injured my feelings. I get hurt when you talk to me like that." But sometimes appeals are not enough. Your partner can't or won't hear you, is defensive, or is in an egocentric frame of mind. That is when you might need rules and structure. When nothing else works, you need rules. But rules should be about connecting, not punishing.

If your connection is being hurt by your mate's behavior or attitudes, and if words aren't working, call in the rules. Protect yourself and preserve the love you want to have. Here are some guidelines to consider:

Bring in a third party. Most people need to talk to someone, like a safe and responsible friend, to process what is going on. Seeing what the problem is, what exactly needs to change, what rules will help, and how to deal with your own anxiety—it is very difficult to do all this in your own head. You need to borrow the head of a wise and trusted friend. Talk to someone who is balanced and *for* the relationship.

Base the rules on the relationship. When you decide what you are going to do, appeal to the connection. Make it clear that this is not about wanting to change or fix your partner. It is because you want to trust and love him or her—but you can't because of a certain behavior pattern or communication tactic. Always come back to the goal: *I am doing this because I want you, and I want us.* If you need a lot of support from sources other than your partner, don't hesitate to get it. You are seeking that support so you can solve this issue and reconnect with your loved one.

Follow through. If rules are needed, set them and live them. If you are afraid you won't follow through, stop and get more resources and help, or you will make things worse for the two of you. Giving in to your feelings or your partner's pleas destroys the effectiveness of the treatment by showing that bad behavior has no consequences.

think about it | talk about it | live it

1 What current relational rules—unspoken or clearly defined —
  guide your connection right now? Have these rules helped or
  hindered your marriage? Explain.

2 What recurring situation or pattern in your connection might
  benefit from relational rules? Some examples are emotional
  unavailability, control, irresponsibility, defensiveness, chronic
  tardiness, overspending, unfaithfulness, rage. How might a
  rule strengthen your connection?

great marriage commitment 20

*With God's help, I will participate in any structure or rules that may help us
avoid hurtful behavior and thus deepen our connection.*

simple secret 21

---

always,
always,
ALWAYS
forgive

It is difficult to rank the twenty-one steps of

this journey in importance, but this last one

is certainly one of the most vital to a great

marriage. Why? Because forgiveness will help

you get through when—notice we said when,

not if—you stumble on the others.

Your ability to connect and reconnect as partners will depend largely on your ability to forgive each other. What is forgiveness? Simply put, forgiveness is when you cancel a debt. It is a word used in legal documents. It assumes that one person has hurt another, and there is a debt to be paid. But forgiveness takes justice in another direction. With forgiveness, *the penalty is cancelled.* There is no punishment. The guilty go free.

Forgiveness is the foundation of the Christian faith. We all have missed the mark, the Bible says. We all owe a debt—one that we cannot pay in full. That predicament is what moved a just and fair God to send His Son to die for our sins, the just for the unjust (1 John 4:10). From this we learn that *forgiveness is the only hope any intimate connection has to grow and flourish.* When one partner incurs the debt, the other feels the pain and knows "I have been wronged." *But he or she lets go of the right to demand justice—and lets the prisoner free*, so to speak, just as God did for us.

The Benefits of Forgiveness

There are strong benefits from building the capacity to forgive into your marriage. Let's take a look at these benefits.

Both partners get another chance. Think about the last time you snapped at your partner or were controlling. How did you want to be handled? Did you want to receive the law, or did you want a chance to be reconnected, loved, and reconciled? Healthy couples realize that they both fail each other and that they need to be given second chances—often.

Grace wins. Your relationship must be fueled by love and grace. When you live in forgiveness with each other, you both experience grace. When you and your mate learn to forgive, you are off the performance track, you are not being judged or condemned, and you are for each other and the relationship. Forgiveness unlocks the grace you both need to keep the connection alive.

The forgiver is free. When you do not forgive, *the hurt still owns you and controls you*. I (John) can think of times in my life in which I was slow to forgive. I brooded. I withdrew. Thoughts, emotions, and memories of the hurt filled my mind. This is not a picture of freedom—it is a prison.

When you cancel your partner's debt, you are free to move ahead and live your life. Forgiveness is a benefit to the wounded party and to the one who does the wounding.

Forgiveness brings gratitude. When you tell your partner, "I forgive you for what you did," you are giving a marvelous gift. You are lifting a burden of condemnation from him or her. In healthy people, this results in a deep and profound sense of gratitude.

You can be real. Couples who forgive don't have to hide their faults from each other, fearing rejection. They are secure enough in the forgiveness to know that they will make it through. So they are real, authentic, and honest with each other. Why hide when you don't have to?

Become a Forgiving Couple

Here are some ways to add the awesome power of forgiveness to your marriage:

Agree on the reality. Agree that you are going to fail each other all throughout your relationship. Agreeing on the reality sets the stage for the need of forgiveness.

Talk about what you want and need. People need different things from their partners regarding forgiveness. One might say, "I just want you to admit it and not excuse it." Another may say, "I want to know you aren't holding something over my head." This dialogue helps you see what needs to happen in your relationship so that both of you can experience the benefits of forgiveness.

Practice receiving and giving forgiveness. Swallow your pride. Phrases like "Will you please forgive me for . . . " and "I forgive you for . . . " need to be part of your normal vocabulary. Using the words, facing each other eyeball to eyeball, brings home the reality of our transgressions and the depth of forgiveness.

Have a "no waiting" policy. When you have a problem, go to your mate as soon as it is realistic and get the forgiveness ball rolling. Do *not* wait for your partner to come to you with an apology. Don't hold on to the offense and bring it up later as ammunition in another argument. Grieve it, feel your sadness, and say good-bye to the right to punish.

We're not saying that you should never bring up or talk about an issue requiring forgiveness. You might have to talk about someone's behavior, selfishness, or irresponsibility if it is an ongoing problem. But talk about it as a problem to be addressed, not as blame from the past.

think about it | talk about it | live it

1 What does forgiveness look like in your relationship? Are you both "on the same page" about forgiveness? Why or why not?

2 Which of the benefits of forgiveness mentioned in this chapter have you personally experienced in your marriage? Which of them do you desire to experience more?

3 Is there an ongoing forgiveness issue you need to address with your mate? Write out what you will say to your mate and set a time to resolve the issue.

great marriage commitment 21

With God's help, I will quickly and gracefully give and seek forgiveness for the inevitable hurts in our relationship.

about the authors

Dr. Henry Cloud and Dr. John Townsend are popular speakers and co-founders of the Cloud-Townsend Clinic and Cloud-Townsend Resources. They are the best-selling authors of the Gold Medallion Award-winning book, *Boundaries*, with more than one million copies sold, as well as numerous other popular titles. Both hold doctorates in clinical psychology and maintain private practices in Southern Califorina.